The Road to Boston: Counterterrorism Challenges and Lessons from the Marathon Bombings

House Homeland Security Committee Report

U.S. House of Representatives
Committee on Homeland Security
Rep. Michael McCaul, Chairman

March 2014

Prepared by the Majority Staff of the Committee on Homeland Security

(U) THE BOSTON MARATHON BOMBING:

(U) AN INVESTIGATIVE REPORT BY THE STAFF OF THE COMMITTEE ON HOMELAND SECURITY

(U) TABLE OF CONTENTS

I.

INTRODUCTION

(U) For over a decade, the United States House of Representatives' Committee on Homeland Security (the Committee) has worked to oversee and strengthen the nation's counterterrorism programs and policies. Established along with the Department of Homeland Security in response to the terrorist attacks of September 11, 2001, the Committee has a responsibility to continually examine our homeland security effort – identifying weaknesses and providing solutions to address these shortfalls.

(U) The Committee's mandate was reemphasized on April 15, 2013, when two improvised explosive devices detonated near the finish line of the 117th Boston Marathon. Krystle Campbell, Martin Richard, and Lu Lingzi died in the attack. Well over two hundred others were injured. The bombs were built with pressure cookers and were packed with shrapnel to inflict maximum damage, in a fashion reportedly popular with militants in Afghanistan and Pakistan. Many lost limbs or suffered other critical injuries, but the true extent of the damage will never be fully recorded. Yet as the Nation and the world looked on – before the smoke had cleared and before they knew it was safe – the citizens of Boston, their police officers and firemen, members of the National Guard, Federal agents, and other spectators, runners, and first responders, rushed forward to help, decisively and honorably.

(U) In the wake of this tragedy, Americans drew inspiration from the example of those heroes. During the hunt for those responsible, Boston once again demonstrated our country's true strength to the world, and proved the futility of horrific violence intended to intimidate Americans.

(U) As the Nation looks forward, it would be a mistake not to reflect on how those responsible were able to carry out their assault in order to prevent similar attacks in the years to come. The Committee has an obligation to conduct such an investigation and, since this attack, has worked toward that end.

(U) The Committee has written multiple letters to Federal agencies, including the Federal Bureau of Investigation (FBI), the Department of Homeland Security (DHS), as well as the Office of the Director of National Intelligence (ODNI), and held several hearings to gather evidence. Committee staff have held multiple briefings with Federal and local officials both in Boston and Washington, and travelled to the Russian Federation to meet with American officials stationed in Moscow and representatives from the Russian government. Unfortunately, while eager to carry out this effort, the Committee initially encountered significant resistance and delays. Yet in recent months, the Committee has received increased cooperation from agencies in the Executive Branch that had previously limited their assistance. The Committee hopes that this more productive relationship can continue not only in relation to this investigation but into all areas of the Committee's jurisdiction.

(U) To conduct our investigation, the Committee repeatedly requested documents and briefings to discuss the specifics of Tamerlan Tsarnaev's history, the extent to which Federal agencies knew about the threat he posed, and what actions they took, or did not take, in response. While some Federal agencies responded to the Committee's questions, for several months the FBI largely denied or ignored the Committee's requests for assistance. In one letter to the Committee, FBI representatives asserted that the Committee's requests amounted to "non-oversight activities" – implying that the FBI was therefore not required to comply.

(U) Despite these challenges, the Committee persisted in working to obtain the required documentation and information. Throughout this effort, the Committee has appreciated the challenges facing the FBI and all other agencies in conducting their investigation into the bombing, and bringing those responsible to justice. The Committee has always applauded the men and women of the FBI, along with all other Federal law enforcement and intelligence officials, and will always endeavor to assist them in their mission.

(U) Yet, just as Federal investigators have a duty to carry out their investigation with speed and integrity, the Committee is obliged to carry out its own investigation – without delay and without leaving any question unanswered – because we do not, and cannot, know when or where the next attack will occur.

(U) Being compelled by our duty to move forward in strengthening our national security, the Committee has decided to release a report that includes findings based on the evidence available to us at present and provide recommendations for further action. The Committee shall consider this an appropriate documentation of our effort to the American people and will endeavor to ensure that the recommendations contained herein are enacted to improve the security of the United States Homeland.

(U) We will also continue to pursue additional information and documentation, and explore all appropriate avenues for fulfilling our mission. As this report will detail, there were opportunities in which greater sharing of information might have altered the course of events. Such failures must not be allowed to persist, and the Committee will continue to work toward strengthening our nation's Homeland Security.

(U) This report was compiled by Committee staff using both classified and unclassified materials, including open source reporting. In many instances, this report utilizes media reporting, in part to address issues raised in news media outlets and in part because initial information about the events was not provided by relevant agencies. A draft version of this document was sent to Federal agencies for review. On December 16, 2013, representatives from the Executive Branch met with Committee staff to discuss this report's classification level and to provide comments on the Committee's findings and recommendations. As such, certain portions of this text have been redacted to preserve the integrity of the sensitive and classified evidence provided to the Committee throughout this investigation. Furthermore, these representatives provided greater insight into steps their agencies have taken to address the issues of concern detailed below. Much of this information is reflected in this report.

(U) The Committee is thankful to all those who assisted in providing evidence and compiling this report, including the Commonwealth of Massachusetts and Boston-area local law enforcement agencies, outside experts, Federal officials, and others. The powerful example of the brave first responders in Boston working to save lives continues to echo in all those who are working to learn from this tragedy. The United States Congress and the American people are appreciative of that effort.

Sincerely,

MICHAEL T. McCAUL
Chairman
Committee on Homeland Security

PETER T. KING
Chairman
Subommittee on Counterterrorism and
Intelligence

WILLIAM R. KEATING

CANDICE S. MILLER
Chairman
Subcommittee on Border and Maritime Security

PATRICK L. MEEHAN
Chairman
Subommittee on Cybersecurity, Infrastructure
Protection and Security Technologies

JEFF DUNCAN
Chairman
Subcommittee on Oversight, Management
and Efficiency

SUSAN W. BROOKS
Chairman
Subcommittee on Emergency Preparedness,
Response, and Communications

RICHARD HUDSON
Chairman
Subcommittee on Transportation Security

II.

EXECUTIVE SUMMARY

(U) This report examines much of Tamerlan Tsarnaev's personal history and his interaction with Federal agencies, including his radicalization, the 2011 threat assessment carried out by the FBI, and his travel to Russia in early 2012. Additionally, the Committee explores missed opportunities that potentially could have prevented this attack.

(U) The Committee has developed seven preliminary recommendations to strengthen our Federal counterterrorism efforts. These recommendations are intended to combat systemic weaknesses the Committee has identified during the course of its investigation, including:

- Insufficient cooperation and information sharing between Federal agencies and local law enforcement;[1]
- Limited communication between Federal agencies;
- Inadequate resources for necessary screening of outbound travelers of interest; and
- Failure to amend inaccurate or incomplete records held by various agencies.

(U) Many of the Committee's recommendations, along with a recommendation to strengthen Congressional oversight of homeland security, echo recommendations included in the 9/11 Commission Report released on July 26, 2004, and are also found in other examinations of terrorist attacks, such as the Senate Homeland Security and Governmental Affairs Committee's review of the Fort Hood shooting. This once again demonstrates that nearly ten years after the release of the findings of the 9/11 Commission, we have yet to fully address these challenges.

(U) **The Committee recommends greater information sharing with local law enforcement, and expanded access to the FBI's classified Guardian system at State and local fusion centers.** In particular, the Committee notes that Joint Terrorism Task Forces (JTTFs) around the country must allow for greater sharing with local police departments and other agencies that sponsor personnel to work on the task forces. **The Committee also recommends that the Memoranda of Understanding between the FBI and other agencies that prevent the sharing of information outside of JTTFs without FBI approval be amended to foster greater sharing.**

(U//FOUO//LES) Additionally, based on classified briefings provided to the Committee, **the Committee will continue its review of efforts by Customs and Border Protection (CBP) to screen outbound travelers who are identified as persons of potential interest.** Based on details provided to the Committee regarding this incident, the Committee supports recent changes in CBP policy ██████████████████████████████████

---

[1] (U) Acknowledging that local law enforcement officials have indicated they may not have done anything differently had they known about the FBI's 2011 assessment on Tamerlan Tsarnaev, in the course of this investigation the Committee has been provided evidence to demonstrate that information sharing remains a problem nontheless.

 The Committee also will work to ensure that CBP has the resources necessary to secure the homeland.

(U//FOUO//LES) Uncertainty continues to surround the question of which Federal agencies and investigators knew of Tamerlan Tsarnaev's travel to Russia. **The Committee recommends requiring detailed records relating to the sharing of ▇▇ records ▇▇▇▇▇▇▇▇▇▇▇▇▇, so that *all* appropriate officials can be reliably informed** ▇▇▇▇▇▇▇▇▇▇▇▇▇▇▇▇▇▇▇▇▇▇▇▇▇▇▇▇▇▇▇▇▇▇▇ If these agencies had proactively communicated with one another and worked to de-conflict their records, each would have had a more thorough picture of the threat Tamerlan Tsarnaev posed, and it could have presented the opportunity to review his case after his return from Dagestan, Russia. **Therefore, the Committee recommends establishing additional requirements to ensure that Federal agencies with information relating to nominations for watch lists proactively communicate with the nominating agencies to ensure all records are full and accurate.** CBP has taken some steps to make these enhancements that will be examined in greater detail below.

(U) In addition to specific policy changes such as those outlined above, the report also identifies broader weaknesses stemming from issues such as public awareness of terrorist threats and government-wide accountability. **To address these, the Committee recommends improving upon programs designed to educate the public about terrorist threats and their role in assisting authorities in identifying and mitigating potential dangers.**

(U) **Finally, the Committee recommends that investigators, analysts, intelligence and law enforcement professionals, and all those charged with guarding the nation's security, continually find new ways to proactively improve our homeland security.** Though difficult to implement, these last two recommendations are perhaps the most important, and the most likely to prevent terrorist attacks in the future. It is difficult to build and evaluate public service and information campaigns, but often, it is the public that is first to notice indicators of an individual's radicalization, plans to commit a terrorist attack, or other signs of danger. It is perhaps even more difficult to build a self-critical bureaucracy, and improve the efficacy of examinations into terror attacks. However, recognizing the limitations of Federal agencies in mitigating terrorist threats is the first step to improving our efforts.

(U) The Committee hopes these recommendations strengthen the hand of Federal, State and local law enforcement, as well as the Intelligence Community, in combating terrorist threats. Though it will never be realistic to expect we can eradicate the threat posed by terrorist networks and the danger of homegrown extremists, the United States should always endeavor to improve our security and these recommendations are a step in that direction.

III.

(U) BACKGROUND AND HISTORY

(U) Terror in the Caucasus

(U) Russia's North Caucasus region has been volatile for decades, as violent Islamist groups in Chechnya, Dagestan, and other neighboring republics have engaged in a ruthless and bloody war against the Russian Federation.[2] Varying assessments suggest that beyond their attacks against the Russian state, these terrorist networks have the potential to cooperate in al Qaeda's global jihad.[3] The current Emir of al Qaeda, Ayman al-Zawahiri was reportedly arrested in Dagestan in 1996, and has also called for the Caucasus to be a jihadist safe haven. Al-Zawahiri noted in 2001,

> (U) *The liberation of the Caucasus would constitute a hotbed of jihad (or fundamentalism as the United States describes it) and that region would become the shelter of thousands of Muslim mujahideen from various parts of the Islamic world, particularly Arab parts. This poses a direct threat to the United States, represented by the growing support for the jihadist movement everywhere in the Islamic world.[4]*

(U) Chechen fighters have also reportedly fought alongside al Qaeda and Taliban forces in Afghanistan.[5] In addition, some estimate that as many as 850 Chechen fighters belong to the Jaish al-Muhajireen wal Ansar – a group of Islamist fighters in Syria allied with al Qaeda's Islamic State of Iraq and the Levant.[6] According to one expert, the Caucasus Emirate (also known as the Imirate Kavkas or IK), the leading violent Islamist extremist group in that region,

---

[2] **(U)** Jim Nichol, "Russian Political, Economic, and Security Issues and U.S. Interests," *the Congressional Research Service*, September 13, 2013.

[3] (U) The FBI noted in an interagency briefing to Committee staff on December 16, 2013 that after the fall of the Soviet Union, "There were two factions to the Chechen resistance movement – Chechen nationalists and jihadists – but for both factions the focus was entirely on Chechen independence."

[4] **(U)** Lorenzo Vidino, "How Chechnya became a Breeding Ground for Terror," *Middle East Quarterly*, September 2005. (Available at: http://www.meforum.org/744/how-chechnya-became-a-breeding-ground-for-terror-#_ftnref1)

[5] **(U)** Michael Heath, and Khalid Qayum, "Pakistan Says Uzbek, Chechen Fighters Aiding Taliban in Swat," *Bloomberg News*, May 21, 2009. (Available at: http://www.bloomberg.com/apps/news?pid=newsarchive&sid=a_Dh7ZyHByps)

[6] **(U)** Mairbek Vathagaev, "Influence of Chechen Leader of North Caucasian Fighters in Syria Grows," *Jamestown Foundation*, August 9, 2013. (Available at: http://www.jamestown.org/single/?no_cache=1&tx_ttnews%5Btt_news%5D=41255&tx_ttnews%5BbackPid%5D=381&cHash=29f5982933f249d513ffd0fd9e3e30853.UIXYVLHD-UI)

has increasingly developed ties with al Qaeda.[7] On May 26, 2011, the United States Department of State added the Caucasus Emirate to the Foreign Terrorist Organization (FTO) list,[8] and the United Nations lists them among entities associated with al Qaeda, noting that they are active in Afghanistan and Pakistan, as well as Russia.[9]

(U) It has not been determined whether the Boston Marathon bombing that took place on April 15, 2013 is tied directly to the Caucasus Emirate or the ongoing terrorist activity in Dagestan, Chechnya, and across the North Caucasus. However, it is reasonable to assume that Tamerlan Tsarnaev was at least inspired by their activity and ideology, and driven to take part in the vision of global jihad which they share with al Qaeda. During Tamerlan Tsarnaev's time in Dagestan, which will be explored in greater detail below, he would have seen Russia's fight against these groups first-hand, and (though Federal investigators have not found proof of these meetings) possibly had the opportunity to meet with rebel fighters from that region, which may have helped to fuel his radicalization. As Secretary of State John Kerry noted in Brussels shortly after the bombing, "[Tamerlan] learned something where he went and came back with a willingness to kill people."[10] Clearly, understanding the context of the situation in the Caucasus sheds some light on Tamerlan Tsarnaev's drive to carry out this attack.

(U) *The Tsarnaev Family*

(U) The Tsarnaev family is ethnic Chechen, though Tamerlan Tsarnaev was born in 1986 in Kyrgyzstan, where his parents lived at the time.[11] While there, Tamerlan Tsarnaev's father, Anzor Tsarnaev, worked for the government of Kyrgyzstan, and in 1993 had a second son, Dzhokhar Tsarnaev. After losing his job in the Kyrgyz Republic in 2001, Anzor Tsarnaev and his family returned to Dagestan – a semi-autonomous Russian republic bordering Chechnya.

(U) In 2002, Anzor Tsarnaev applied for asylum in the United States after previously being granted a tourist visa.[12] The Tsarnaev parents and Dzhokhar Tsarnaev arrived first, leaving

---

[7] **(U)** Gordon Hahn, "Getting the Caucasus Emirate Right," *The Center for Strategic and International Studies*, August 2011.

[8] **(U)** Office of the Spokesman, "Designation of the Caucasus Emirate," *U.S. Department of State*, May 26, 2011. (Available at: http://www.state.gov/r/pa/prs/ps/2011/05/164312.htm)

[9] **(U)** 1267 Committee, "Al-Qaida Sanctions List," *the United Nations*, October 1, 2013.

[10] **(U)** Tracy Jan, Globe Staff, "Secretary of State John Kerry Says Tamerlan Tsarnaev Returned from Russia 'with a willingness to kill people'" *The Boston Globe*, April 24, 2013. (Available at: http://www.boston.com/politicalintelligence/2-13/04/24/secretary-state-john-kerry-says-tamerlan-tsarnaev-returned-from-russia-with-willingness-kill-people/T4BzsQN7iRMbEZbfmA5NbP/story.html)

[11] **(U)** CNN Staff, "Timeline: A look at Tamerlan Tsarnaev's past," *CNN*, April 22, 2013. (Available at: http://edition.cnn.com/2013/04/21/us/tamerlan-tsarnaev-timeline/index.html)

[12] **(U)** Glenn Kessler, "Rand Paul's misguided question on how the Tsarnaev brothers arrived in the United States," *the Washington Post*, April 23, 2013. (Available at: http://www.washingtonpost.com/blogs/fact-checker/post/rand-pauls-misguided-question-on-how-the-tsarnaev-brothers-arrived-in-the-united-states/2013/04/22/095ec08c-ab9d-11e2-a8b9-2a63d75b5_blog.html)

Tamerlan Tsarnaev and his sisters in an uncle's care for another year.[13] Subsequently, in 2003, Tamerlan Tsarnaev and his sisters joined their family in the United States.[14] In 2006, Tamerlan Tsarnaev was granted Lawful Permanent Resident (LPR) status. By this time, he had taken up boxing, and in the fall of 2006 he attended Bunker Hill Community College part-time. He left the school in 2008.[15]

(U) In 2007, Tamerlan Tsarnaev began dating Katherine Russell.[16] According to some media reporting, friends of Katherine Russell claim that as time went on he took on an increasingly extremist view of Islam, and allege that he became violent toward her. During a break in their relationship, Tamerlan Tsarnaev was arrested on charges of domestic abuse for slapping a different woman, Nadine Ascencao.[17] In 2009, he won the New England Golden Gloves heavyweight title, and lost in the first round of the national tournament in Salt Lake City. The next year, though he qualified for the national tournament, he was not allowed to compete due to a change in the competition's rules. Tamerlan Tsarnaev married Katherine Russell on June 21, 2010.[18] His daughter, Zahira, was born in October 2010.

(U) For his part, Dzhokhar Tsarnaev attended high school at the Cambridge Rindge and Latin School in Cambridge, Massachusetts where he wrestled competitively and eventually became co-captain of the wrestling team.[19] In 2011, he graduated and received a $2,500 scholarship from the City of Cambridge for college, which he used to attend the University of Massachusetts at Dartmouth.[20] His grades were poor, but by nearly all public accounts he was well-liked and social, and was known to drink and smoke marijuana with friends. He also reportedly maintained a close relationship with his older brother. On September 11, 2012, Dzhokhar became a naturalized U.S. citizen.[21]

---

[13] (U) CNN Staff, *supra* note 11.

[14] (U) It is important to note that despite conflicting early reports, the Tsarnaev family received asylum from Kyrgyzstan, and not Russia.

[15] (U) CNN Staff, *supra* note 11.

[16] (U) Philip Caulfield, "Tamerlan Tsarnaev abused Katherine Russell with taunts of 'slut' and 'prostitute' during courtship: roommates," *New York Daily News*, April 23, 2013. (Available at: http://nydailynews.com/news.national/tamerlan-tsarnaev-abused-katherine-russell-taunts-slut-prostitute-courtship-roommates-article-1.1325216#ixzz2RaDpoCzcNewYork)

[17] (U) Chris Krik and Heather Brady, "From Boxing Champion to Bombing Suspect," *Slate*, April 25, 2013. (Available at: http://www.slate.com/articles_news_and_politics/map_of_the_week/2013/04/timeline_boston_bombing_suspect_tamerlan_tsarnaev_s_life.html)

[18] (U) Jack Gillum, Katie Zezima and Michelle R. Smith, "Talented Rhode Island artisit married to bombing suspect Tamerlan Tsarnaev," *the Associated Press*, April 22, 2013. (Available at: http://www.masslive.com/news/index/ssf/2013/04/katherine-russell_tamerlan-tsa.html)

[19] (U) Chris Krik and Heather Brady, *supra* note 17.

[20] (U) Ibid.

[21] (U) Ibid.

(U) The Tsarnaev family struggled with money during their time in the United States.[22] Anzor Tsarnaev worked as an auto mechanic. Tamerlan Tsarnaev's mother, Zubeidat Tsarnaeva, worked multiple jobs over the years to help make ends meet, including time as a cosmetologist and an in-home care taker.[23] In June 2012 she was allegedly caught shoplifting from a store in Natick, Massachusetts.[24] Zubeidat and Anzor Tsarnaev are reportedly separated, though both returned to Russia before the Boston Marathon bombing.[25]

(U) *2011 Assessment of Tamerlan Tsarnaev*

(U) In 2011, the FBI received a letter from the Russian Federal Security Service (FSB) regarding Tamerlan Tsarnaev.[26] In the letter, the Russian government expressed concern that he had become radicalized and that he might return to Russia and join extremist groups there.[27] While lacking compelling derogatory information on exactly why he posed a threat, the letter contained detailed biographic information on Tamerlan Tsarnaev and his mother, including physical addresses, marital status, online social media profiles, and discussed his history as a boxer. The letter also noted that he had previously hoped to travel to the Palestinian territories to wage jihad, but decided not to go because he did not speak Arabic. The letter requested that the FBI notify the Russian government if Tamerlan Tsarnaev attempted to travel to Russia, which may indicate they were concerned about possible ties to militants in the Caucasus.

(U) In response to this letter, the FBI Joint Terrorism Task Force (JTTF) in Boston initiated an assessment to determine if Tamerlan Tsarnaev did indeed pose a terrorist threat. Such threat assessments are outlined in the Attorney General Guidelines for Domestic FBI Operations,

---

[22] (U) Alan Cullison, Paul Sonne, and Jennifer Levitz, "Life in America Unraveled for Brothers," *the Wall Street Journal,* April 20, 2013. (Available at: http://onlinewsj.com/article/SB10001421278873238093045784325014352232278.hjtml)

[23] (U) Alan Cullison, "Boston Bombing Suspect Was Steeped in Conspiracies," *the Wall Street Journal* http://stream.wsj.com/story/latest-headlines/SS-2-63399/SS-2-294822/)

(U) Erik Ortiz, "Zubeidat Tsarnaeva, mom of alleged Boston bombers, became increasingly stricter in Islamic faith," *the New York Daily News,* April 23, 2013. (Available at: http://nydailynews.com/news/crime/tsarnaev-matriarch-stricter-islamic-faith-article-1.1325208)

[24] (U) Daily Mail Reporter, "Mother of Boston bombing suspects arrested last year for 'stealing $1,600 worth of clothes from Lord and Taylor," *the Daily Mail,* April 19, 2013. (Available at: http:dailymail.co.uk/news/article-2311653/Boston-bombings-Mother-Boston-bombing-suspects-arrested-year-stealing-1-600-worth-clothes-Lord--Taylor.html)

[25] (U) Alan Cullison, Paul Sonne, and Jennifer Levitz, *supra* note 22.

[26] (U) Kathy Lally, "Russian FSB Describes its Tsarnaev Letter to FBI," *Washington Post,* May 31, 2013. (Available at: http://articles.washingtonpost.com/2013-05-31/world/39656209_1_dagestan-keating-tamerlan-tsarnaev)

[27] (S//FGI//NF) Russian FSB Liaison Memorandum to FBI (Access provided to the Committee courtesy of the House of Representatives Committee on the Judiciary), March 4, 2011

along with preliminary investigations and investigations. Each of these respective categories of investigative activity increases in scope, with assessments being the least intrusive. In the course of their inquiry, the Boston JTTF checked U.S. government databases and other information to look for such things as derogatory telephone communications, possible use of online sites associated with the promotion of radical activity, associations with other persons of interest, travel history and plans, and education history. No links to terrorism were uncovered in these records checks and investigation of Tamerlan Tsarnaev's background. The investigators then interviewed his parents and Tamerlan Tsarnaev himself. The FBI did not find any evidence of terrorist activity, and this information was provided to the Russian government in the summer of 2011.[28]

(U//FOUO//LES) The FBI Case Agent on the Boston JTTF had the Customs and Border Protection (CBP) Officer assigned to his team enter a TECS record in order to provide notification of Tamerlan Tsarnaev's international travel.[29] TECS is owned and managed by CBP and is its principal law enforcement and anti-terrorism database. TECS is established as an overarching law enforcement information collection, analysis, and sharing environment. TECS contains Department of Homeland Security (DHS) immigration data, as well as information from other government, criminal and terrorism databases, including information from the Terrorist Screening Database (frequently referred to as "the watchlist" or TSDB). TECS also provides the ability to query the National Crime Information Center (NCIC), and the National Law Enforcement Telecommunications System (NLETS).

(U//FOUO//LES) TECS records may be generated on individuals of interest in order to identify international travel and/or request specific actions upon encounter.

(U//FOUO//LES) In this case, the alert was placed on March 22, 2011 and revised two days later.[30] The alert provided contact information for the FBI agent leading the investigation into Tamerlan Tsarnaev and requested that the agent be notified of Tamerlan Tsarnaev's international travel.

---

[28] (U) "2011 Request for Information on Tamerlan Tsarnaev from Foreign Government," *FBI National Press Office*, April 19, 2013. (Available at: http://www.fbi.gov/news/pressrel/press-releases/2011-request-for-information-on-tamerlan-tsarnaev-from-foreign-government)

[29] (U) Previously known as the Treasury Enforcement Communications System, this program is now officially referred to as TECS.

[30] (U) Tamerlan Tsarnaev's TECS Records Supplied to the Committee

[REDACTED] [31] However, though this alert was still active at the time of his departure, Tamerlan Tsarnaev did not receive the requested screening. The Committee will elaborate on this issue in greater detail below, however [REDACTED] there is no evidence that CBP officials at the John F. Kennedy International Airport examined his TECS record as a result of his listing. [33] Therefore, they would not have seen this explicit request.

(U) After the FBI's assessment of Tamerlan Tsarnaev found no links to terrorism, the Boston JTTF officially closed their assessment on June 24, 2011. [34] In the summer of 2011, the FBI notified the Russian government that they had reviewed Tamerlan Tsarnaev and identified no links to terrorism. [35] The FBI also requested that the Russian government provide "more specific or additional information" that would indicate why Tamerlan Tsarnaev posed a threat. Federal officials have stated that the Russian government did not reply. [36]

(U) Tamerlan *Tsarnaev's Travel to Russia*

(U//FOUO) Tamerlan Tsarnaev traveled to Russia in January 2012, and returned to the U.S. in July 2012. Federal investigators are still working to piece together details of his visit, but FBI officials stationed at the U.S. Embassy in Moscow informed the Committee that before Anzor Tsarnaev arrived in Russia in May 2012, Tamerlan Tsarnaev spent time with other family in Makhachkala. [37] There are conflicting media reports regarding the amount of time they spent together and the possibility that they may have travelled to other areas during the visit – either to

---

[31] (U)Tamerlan Tsarnaev's TECS Records Supplied to the Committee

[32] (U) U.S. Customs and Border Protection, "CBP Outbound Screening Briefing Follow Up Questions," provided to the Committee on December 23, 2013.

[33] (U) The Committee will elaborate on steps CBP is taking to address this issue below.

[34] (U) DHS Briefings to Committee Staff, June 2013.

[35] (U) *FBI National Press Office, supra* note 28.

[36] (U) Ibid.

[37] (U) A delegation of Committee staff traveled to the region, and spoke with U.S. officials at the embassies in Moscow and Tbilisi. Committee staff were briefed by FBI officials in advance of an anticipated third and final round of investigative interviews relating to the FBI's criminal investigation into the Boston Marathon bombing.

other parts of Dagestan or into Chechnya.[38] While the facts presently known about Tamerlan Tsarnaev's travel do not indicate that this attack has connections to an external terror network, they do raise significant questions. For example, it is possible that Tamerlan Tsarnaev's travel provided him with an opportunity to make contact with militants in the region. Tamerlan Tsarnaev also reportedly prayed at the al-Nadira mosque during his time in Makhachkala.[39] Writing for *The Wall Street Journal*, Alan Cullison alleges that the mosque's founder, Nadirshakh Khachilaev, also aided Ayman al Zawahiri, "during a 1997 trip to Dagestan."[40] Furthermore, some media accounts report that while in Dagestan, Tamerlan Tsarnaev made contact with Mahmoud Mansour Nidal, a known insurgent in the region, and perhaps others.[41]

(U) Mahmoud Nidal was reportedly a recruiter for Islamist insurgents in Dagestan and some media reporting suggests he and Tamerlan Tsarnaev could have met several times in 2012.[42] Though on the run from Russian authorities during much of Tamerlan Tsarnaev's time in Dagestan, a former Russian investigator familiar with Mahmoud Nidal noted that he would probably not have been afraid to emerge from hiding and that the two could have met.[43] Mahmoud Nidal was killed in a raid by Russian forces on May 19, 2012.

(U) In January 2014 Chairman McCaul and Representative William Keating traveled to Russia and met with investigative journalists who had spent time in Makhachkala, Dagestan, looking into Tamerlan Tsarnaev's time there. These sources reported that he had attempted to join the Chechen fighters, and met with Mahmoud Nidal. These sources further allege that Tamerlan Tsarnaev was rejected by these groups, in part because of his conspicuously Western style.

(U//FOUO) However, according to briefings provided to Committee staff by officials at the U.S. Embassy in Moscow, official investigators have uncovered no evidence of such a relationship between Mahmoud Nidal and Tamerlan Tsarnaev. Furthermore, investigators have

---

[38] (U) Miriam Elder, "Tamerlan Tsarnaev in Dagestan: the unanswered questions," *The Guardian*, April 22, 2013. (Available at: http://guardian.co.uk/world/2013/apr/22/tamerlan-tsarnaev-dagestan-boston-bombings)

[39] (U) James Brooke, "Boston Bomber Spent 6 Months in Russia's Most Violent Republic," *Voice of America News*, May 20, 2013. (Available at: http://www.voanews.com/content/tsarnaev-dagestan-russia-ties-may-hold-valuable-clues/1664419.html)

[40] (U) Alan Cullison, "Dagestan Islamists Were Uneasy About Boston Bombing Suspect," *Wall Street Journal*, May 9, 2013. (Available at: http://online.wsj.com/news/articles/SB10001424127887324059704578473160866108832)

[41] (U) Jake Tapper, Jessica Metzger, Sherisse Pham, "Russian sources tell congressman Boston suspect met with two Chechen extremists," the Lead with Jake Tapper, *CNN*, May 9, 2013. (Available at: http://thelead.blogs.cnn.com/2013/05/09/russian-sources-tellcongressman-boston-suspect-met-with-two-chechen-extremists/)

[42] (U) Simon Shuster, "A Dead Militant in Dagestan: Did This Slain Jihadi Meet Tamerlan Tsarnaev," *TIME*, May 1, 2013. (Available at: http://world.time.com/2013/05/01/a-dead-militant-in-dagestan-did-this-slain-jihadi-meet-tamerlan-tsarnaev/)

[43] (U) Ibid.

determined Tamerlan Tsarnaev likely did not attempt "go into the forest" – a euphemism for to joining Chechen rebel groups.

(U) According to at least one Russian media report, Tamerlan Tsarnaev has also been linked to Canadian extremist William Plotnikov during his time in the North Caucasus.[44] Writing for the Russian paper *Novaya Gazzetta*, journalist Irina Gordienko alleges that Russian authorities were first alerted to Tamerlan Tsarnaev after finding evidence of "frequent contacts" between the two on William Plotnikov's computer.[45] Though born in Russia, William Plotnikov grew up in Canada and, like Tamerlan Tsarnaev, took up competitive boxing.[46] He converted to Islam in 2009 and left Canada to join rebels in Dagestan less than a year later.[47] William Plotnikov died during a shootout with Russian security services on July 14, 2012.[48]

(S//FGI//NF) FBI officials in Moscow indicated that electronic communication between the two may have been collected ████████████████████████████ ███████ These officials also reported that investigators have determined it is unlikely the two met face-to-face while Tamerlan Tsarnaev was in Dagestan.

(U) *Early Warnings*

(U) While the many specific details of Tamerlan Tsarnaev's radicalization remain somewhat vague, some known details begin to paint a picture. A YouTube account under his name showed that he viewed multiple Russian-language videos on Islam and even compiled playlists of jihadi videos. This account was created only a few weeks after Tamerlan Tsarnaev's return to the U.S., possibly indicating some degree of radicalization had taken place while he was in Russia. One 13-minute video entitled "The Emergence of Prophecy: The Black Flags of Khorasan" details a jihadi prophecy that at the end of the world, a holy army will rise out of a region historically associated with Afghanistan, and sweep across the Middle East to Jerusalem.[49]

(U) One playlist also included a video, since deleted, entitled "Rabbanikaly Amir Abu Dujana – Appeal to the Militias."[50] That name is reportedly the alias of the Dagestani terrorist

---

[44] (U) Fatima Tilsova, "Russians Closely Monitored Boston Bombing Suspect," *Voice of America News*, May 7, 2013. (Available at: http://www.voanews.com/content/tsarnaev-dagestan-bombing/1656176.html)

[45] (U) Ibid.

[46] (U) Simon Shuster, "The Boston-Bomber Trail: Fresh Clues in Rural Dagestan," *TIME*, April 29, 2013. (Available at: http://world.time.com/2013/04/29/picking-up-the-boston-bomber-trail-in-utamysh-russia/)

[47] (U) Stewart Bell, "The Canadian who converted to jihad: Boxer turned militant killed in Dagestan," *National Post*, August 20, 2012. (Available at: http://news.nationalpost.com/2012/08/20/dagestan/)

[48] (U) Ibid.

[49] (U) Video available at:
https://www.youtube.com/watch?v=uJknGtKV34I&list=PLPuUsYCtPwgb_NBDcY2PdenExr6BFSrz&index=6

[50] (U) Tamerlan Tsarnaev YouTube account. (Available at: https://www.youtube.com/user/muazseyfullah)

Gadzhimurad Dolgatov, who was killed in December 2012.[51] Dolgatov was based out of Kizilyurt, a town 40 miles away from Makhachkala, the capital of Dagestan, where Tamerlan Tsarnaev stayed during his trip in early 2012.[52] There is no evidence that Tamerlan Tsarnaev and Dolgatov met, however it appears Tamerlan Tsarnaev was intrigued by the jihadist rebels in the Caucasus and perhaps inspired by their general ideology.

(U) Tsarnaev family members allege that a man known as "Misha" further shaped Tamerlan Tsarnaev's views, although investigators have dismissed that Misha played a role in this attack. A man claiming to be Misha, whose full name is Mikhail Allakhverdov, insists that while he knew Tamerlan Tsarnaev in 2009, he was not influential in his radicalization.[53]

(U) In a public statement, the Islamic Society of Boston (ISB) Cultural Center reported that Tamerlan Tsarnaev attended prayers at this mosque from time to time.[54] On multiple occasions, he engaged in shouting matches with preachers at the mosque, and was asked to leave. These disputes allegedly arose from Tamerlan accusing the preacher of being a "non-believer" and "hypocrite" who was "contaminating people's minds," for encouraging worshippers to celebrate American holidays. Unfortunately, this information was not shared with the authorities, and therefore did not contribute to what Federal investigators knew about Tamerlan Tsarnaev until made public after the bombing.

(U) At this point, the Committee shall refrain from commenting on Dzhokhar Tsarnaev's potential radicalization out of sensitivity to the ongoing court proceedings relating to his involvement in the Boston Marathon bombing.

[51] (U) Adam Taylor, "The Mystery of Tamerlan Tsarnaev's Trip to Dagestan," *Business Insider*, April 20, 2013. (Available at: http://www.businessinsider.com/tamerlan-tsarnaevs-trip-to-dagestan-2013-4)

[52] (U) Ellen Barry, Andrew Roth, "New York Times Interview with Suspects' Father," *the New York Times*. (Available at: http://thelede.blogs.nytimes.com/2013/04/19/updates-on-aftermath-of-boston-marathon-explosions-2/#new-york-times-interview-with-suspects-father)

[53] (U) James Nye, and David McCormack, "'Misha' Speaks Out: Friend Accused of Radicalizing Boston Bomber is revealed as 39-year-old Islam convert with an U.S. girlfriend as he DENIES Teaching Tamerlan Tsarnaev," the *Daily Mail*, April 28, 2013. (Available at: http://www.dailymail.co.uk/news/article-2316360/Misha-speaks-DENIES-radicalizing-Boston-bomber-Tamerlan-Tsarnaev.html)

[54] (U) Associated Press, "Tamerlan Tsarnaev mosque outbursts described," *Politico*, April 22, 2013. (Available at: http://www.politico.com/story/2013/04/tamerlan-tsarnaev-mosque-outburst-described-90474.html)

IV.

(U) THE BOSTON MARATHON BOMBING

(U) *April 15, 2013*

(U) On Monday, April 15, 2013, at roughly 2:50 p.m., two explosions occurred near the finish line of the Boston Marathon.[55] Within moments, first responders, including local law enforcement, Federal agents and emergency medical technicians (EMTs), as well as volunteer medical personnel on scene were securing the area and tending to those injured in the blast. Though initial casualty estimates varied, the attack resulted in three deaths and approximately 260 injuries. Initial reports suggested possible additional explosives, in particular at the John F. Kennedy Presidential Library, but those reports were ultimately deemed inaccurate.[56] Following the blasts, a unit from the Massachusetts Army National Guard posted near the marathon route to provide security for the race immediately began "removing debris and providing medical assistance."[57] According to one report, over 400 Guardsmen on-duty at the marathon responded to the bombing and stayed on duty throughout the day to assist law enforcement.[58] Over 1,500 Guardsmen were activated in response to the incident in the first 24 hours following the blasts.[59] One group of guardsmen helped to set up a Joint Incident Site Communications Capability (JISCC), allowing the emergency responders on site access to computers and telephones.[60]

(U) Shortly after the attack, the Boston Police Department (BPD) detained a Saudi national who was reportedly behaving suspiciously near the site of the explosions. This individual was questioned for nearly five hours and voluntarily allowed BPD officers, as well as FBI and Bureau of Alcohol, Tobacco, Firearms, and Explosives (ATF) agents to search his

---

[55] **(U)** Keith Herbert, "Boston Marathon timeline: from attack to capture," *Newsday*, April 20, 2013. (Available at: http://www.newsday.com/news/nation/boston-marathon-timeline-from-attack-to-capture-1.5112336)

[56] **(U)** Ibid.

[57] **(U)** Brian Naylor, "Boston Response Praised, But Intelligence-Sharing Questioned," *National Public Radio*, April 24, 2013. (Available at: http://www.npr.org/2013/04/24/178815160/boston-response-praised-but-intelligence-sharing-questioned)

[58] **(U)** "Around the Army: Mass. National Guard supports Boston Police Force," *Bayonet & Saber*, April 16, 2013. (Available at: http://www.thebayonet.com/2013/04/17/418061.html#storylink=cpy)

[59] **(U)** Cynthia Simison, "Massachusetts National Guard Gen. Scott Rice says upwards of 1,500 troops on duty to support Boston in wake of marathon bombings," *The Republican*, April 16, 2013. (Available at: http://www.masslive.com/news/index.ssf/2013/04/masssachusett_national_guard_g.html)

[60] **(U)** Susan L. Ruth, "First Responders, National Guard at Boston Marathon," *the Washington Times*, April 25, 2013. (Available at: http://communities.washingtontimes.com /neighborhood/political-potpurri/2013/apr/25/first-responders-national-guard-save-lives-boston-/#ixzz2RUyEWRnX)

apartment. Although his actions and the resulting questioning led to speculation regarding his involvement, the Saudi national was later confirmed by BPD not to be a suspect.[61]

(U) Immediately following the explosion the FBI, Massachusetts State Police (MSP), local police, and ATF began investigating the attack.[62] At 4:50 p.m., the Federal Aviation Administration (FAA) issued a ground stop for Boston Logan International Airport, and restricted the airspace over the site of the explosion.[63] Concurrently, investigators examined video and photographs of the marathon route from before, during, and after the bombing.[64]

(U) *The Manhunt*

(U) Days into the investigation, Federal investigators identified video evidence of the suspects they believed responsible, and eventually turned to the public in an effort to pinpoint the identities of the unknown individuals. At 5:10 p.m. on Thursday, April 18, 2013, investigators released pictures of the two suspects, later identified as the Tsarnaev brothers.[65] This touched off a day-long manhunt and Boston-area citizens were later asked to remain in their homes throughout the following day. The FBI's Special Agent in Charge (SAC), Richard Deslauriers, warned the public that the suspects were considered "to be armed and extremely dangerous."[66] Around 10:30 p.m. on April 18, 2013, Massachusetts Institute of Technology (MIT) campus police officer Sean Collier was found with multiple gunshot wounds and pronounced dead at Massachusetts General Hospital. Investigators believe that the Tsarnaev brothers killed Officer Collier in order to steal his gun.[67]

---

[61] (U) O'Ryan Johnson, Laurel J. Sweet, "Roommate: Cops searched home of Saudi student injured by shrapnel," The Boston Herald, April 16, 2013. (Available at: http://bostonherald.com/news_opinion/local_coverage/2013/04/roommate_cops_searched_home_of_saudi_student_injured_by_shrapnel)

[62] (U) David Abel, Travis Anderson, Martin Finucane, "Three killed, including 8-year old boy, in explosions at Boston Marathon Finish Line; President Obama vows to bring perpetrators to justice," *the Boston Globe*, April 16, 2013. (Available at: http://www.boston.com/metrodesk/2013/04/15/explosions-rock-boston-marathon-finish-line-dozens-injured/UyiedznUFjQRjOKwTXuSDL/story.html)

[63] (U) Nancy Trejos, "FAA lifts ground stop at Boston Logan," *USA Today*, April 16, 2013. (Available at: http://www.usatoday.com/story/todayinthesky/2013/04/15/bostn-marathon-logan-airport/2085871/)

[64] (U) Mark Hosenball, Svea Herbst-Bayliss, "Investigators scour video, photos for Boston Marathon bomb clues," *Reuters*, April 15, 2013. (Available at: http://www.reuters.com/article/2013/04/16/us-athletics-marathon-boston-blast-invest-idUSBRE93F03Y20130416)

[65] (U) J.M. Hirsch, "Boston Bombing Overview: The Unfolding of A 5-Day Manhunt For Suspects," *Huffington Post*, April 21, 2013. (Available at: http://www.huffington post.com/2013/04/21/boston-bombing-timeline_n_3127079.html)

[66] (U) Ibid.

[67] (U) "The Hunt for the Boston Bombing Suspects," *the New York Times*, April 19, 2013. (Available at: http://www.nytimes.com/interactive/2013/04/19/us/boston-marathon-manhunt.html?_r=0)

(U) Shortly afterwards, a man reported to police that he had been carjacked at gunpoint by two males.[68] According to some media accounts, using the stolen-vehicle's built-in GPS system, law enforcement personnel were able to catch up to the suspects in Watertown, a suburb of Boston.[69] Officers of the Watertown Police Department (WPD) approached the vehicle unaware that the suspects in the car theft were also the bombers. The suspects exchanged gunfire with police and threw improvised explosives, including pipe bombs and pressure cooker bombs, from their vehicle.[70] Massachusetts Bay Transit Authority (MBTA) Officer Richard Donohue was critically wounded after being shot. Though shot several times during the gunfight, Tamerlan Tsarnaev charged officers and taunted them repeatedly. WPD Officers were able to apprehend him after he threw his gun at an officer after it either ran out of ammunition or malfunctioned.[71]

(U) As Tamerlan Tsarnaev was being apprehended his brother, Dzhokhar Tsarnaev, sped at the officers in the carjacked vehicle. Sergeant Jeffrey Pugliese attempted to pull Tamerlan Tsarnaev out of the way, and later reported, "I grabbed Tamerlan by the waist of his pants. I was trying to pull him out of the street... I had my prisoner; I didn't want anything to happen to him at this point. The next thing I knew, the headlights were right here in my face, and I had to let go of Tamerlan."[72] Dzhokhar Tsarnaev's vehicle reportedly struck his brother as he sped off, yet the fatally wounded Tamerlan Tsarnaev still struggled to resist being put into handcuffs. Some accounts suggest that Tamerlan Tsarnaev may also have been dragged a short distance by his brother's vehicle. After being taken to Beth Israel Deaconess Medical Center, Tamerlan Tsarnaev died at approximately 1:35 a.m., April 19, 2013.[73]

(U) Dzhokhar Tsarnaev abandoned the vehicle in Watertown and escaped on foot.[74] At 4:30 a.m., MSP and BPD personnel held a news conference in which they told residents of eastern Watertown to remain in their homes, while police officers and FBI agents began

[68] (U) Chelsea J. Carter and Greg Botelho, "'CAPTURED!!!' Boston Police announce Marathon bombing suspect in custody," *CNN*, April 19, 2013. (Available at: http://www.cnn.com/2013/04/19/us/boston-area-violence/index.html)

[69] (U) Vincent DeWitt, "EXCLUSIVE: Watertown Mass. Police describe takedown of Boston Marathon Bombers," *the New York Post*, July 8, 2013. (Available at: http://nypost.com/2013/07/08/exclusive-mass-police-takedown-of-boston-marathon-bombers/)

[70] (U) Emily Davis, "'They hurled a pressure cooker bomb as a decoy': Eyewitness of Watertown shootout describes 'firefight' between suspects and police as bullets penetrated his apartment" the Daily Mail, April 19, 2013. (Available at: http://www.dailymail.co.uk/news/article-2311551/Watertown-shootout-eyewitness-describes-pressure-cooker-bomb-used-decoy-firefight-police-Boston-marathon-terror-suspects.html)

[71] (U) Vincent DeWitt, *supra* note 69.

[72] (U) Ibid.

[73] (U) Liz Kowalczyk, "Beth Israel Staff tried to revive suspect," *the Boston Globe*, April 20, 2013. (Available at: http://www.bostonglobe.com/lifestyle/health-wellness/2013/04/19/beth-israel-deaconess-medical-staff-tried-revive-suspect-killed-shootout/EklhnOS3cRiFmrWSBcje5O/story.html)

[74] (U) "The Hunt for the Boston Bombing Suspects," *the New York Times*, April 19, 2013. (Available at: http://www.nytimes.com/interactive/2013/04/19/us/boston-marathon-manhunt.html?_r=0)

searching for Dzhokhar. By 5:50 a.m., authorities expanded their request for residents to shelter in place to Watertown, Newton, Waltham, Belmont, Cambridge, Arlington and the Allston-Brighton neighborhoods of Boston. At the same time, all Boston area mass transit was shut down.[75] With Watertown and the surrounding areas on lockdown, police initiated a door-to-door search for Dzhokhar Tsarnaev. At a press conference at 12:30 p.m., MSP stated that they had searched over "60 to 70 percent of what we want to cover."[76]

(U) However, around nightfall, police began to scale back the manhunt. At an evening briefing at approximately 6:10 p.m., Massachusetts Governor Deval Patrick announced that the shelter-in-place request had been lifted and that MBTA and other mass transit services would resume immediately.[77] Not long after the lockdown order was lifted, a Watertown resident reported finding a man, covered in blood, in a boat in his backyard and called the police. When officers arrived, they attempted to talk to Dzhokhar Tsarnaev, who was weakened by a gunshot wound he likely received during the overnight shootout with police.[78] The manhunt came to an end when BPD announced at 8:45 p.m. via Twitter that Dzhokhar Tsarnaev was in custody, followed by an announcement from the Mayor of Boston, Thomas Menino, at 8:50 p.m.[79] After being taken into custody, the Department of Justice (DOJ) directed law enforcement to question Dzhokhar Tsarnaev before reading him his Miranda rights, citing an established exception frequently used for questioning about immediate threats to public safety.[80]

(U) Several weeks after the bombing, several media outlets reported that a handwritten note had been scrawled on the interior of the boat in which Dzhokhar Tsarnaev hid on April 19th, 2013. This note allegedly referred to the victims of the Boston Marathon bombings as "collateral damage" and attempted to justify the attacks by saying, "When you attack one Muslim, you attack all Muslims."[81]

(U) Additionally, Dzhokhar Tsarnaev reportedly confirmed to investigators during questioning that he and his brother at one point intended to drive to New York City and detonate

---

[75] (U) "Second Boston Marathon Bombing Suspect Dzhokhar Tsarnaev in Custody," *PBS*, April 19, 2013. (Available at: http://www.pbs.org/newshour/rundown/2013/04/one-boston-marathon-suspect-dead-one-on-the-run-boston-on-lockdown.html)

[76] (U) *The New York Times, supra* note 74.

[77] (U) *PBS, supra* note 75.

[78] (U) J.M. Hirsch, *supra* note 65.

[79] (U) *PBS, supra* note 75.

[80] (U) Eric Schmitt, Michael S. Schmidt, and Ellen Barry, "Bombing Inquiry Turns to Motive and Russia Trip," *the New York Times*, April 20, 2013. (Available at: http://www.nytimes.com/2013/04/21/us/boston-marathon-bombings.html)

[81] (U) Daily Mail Reporter, "'F*** America': Boston 'bomber' scrawled 'confession' on side of boat revealing he would not mourn 'martyr' brother because he was 'in paradise'" *the Daily Mail*, May 16, 2013. (Available at: http://dailymail.co.uk/news/article-2325524/Dzhokhar-Tsarnaev-Boston-bomber-scrawled-F--America -confession-boat.html)

their explosives in Times Square.[82] Fortunately, their shootout with local authorities prevented this from being possible.

(U) *Subsequent Developments in Connection with this Case*

(U) On Wednesday May 1, 2013, investigators announced the arrest of three additional persons associated with Dzhokhar Tsarnaev.[83] One of the individuals, Robel Philipos, a U.S. citizen, has been charged with lying to investigators.[84] Two others, Azamat Tazhayakov and Dias Kadyrbayev, are citizens of Kazakhstan who had come to the United States to attend school.[85] The two are accused of disposing of a backpack and laptop belonging to Dzhokhar Tsarnaev after they realized he might be connected to the bombing, although they claim to have known nothing of the plot beforehand. Azamat Tazhayakov, who attended the University of Massachusetts Dartmouth with Dzhokhar Tsarnaev, returned to the U.S. on January 20, 2013, after a few weeks in Kazakhstan.[86] During that time, he had been dismissed from the University and his student status had been terminated. CBP officials did not prevent him from entering the country because he still held the proper documentation, and they did not check his status in the Student Exchange Visitor Information System (SEVIS).[87] DHS officials report they first addressed this gap by implementing mandatory manual SEVIS screening for all student visa holders entering the country. Now, DHS has implemented automated TECS record placement for all students and exchange visitors that have violated their status or are associated with an invalid SEVIS record.

(U) Another individual, Ibragim Todashev, was questioned by authorities multiple times for his connections with Tamerlan Tsarnaev, under suspicions the two of them may have

---

[82] **(U)** Jerry Markon, Sari Horwitz, and Peter Finn, "Authorities: Tsarnaev Brothers Planned Attack on New York's Times Square," *the New York Times*, April 25, 2013. (Available at: http://www.washingtonpost.com/politics/authorities-tsarnaev-brothers-planned-attack-on-new-yorks-times-square/2013/04/25/5efc342c-add5-11e2-8bf6-e70cb6ae066e_story.html

[83] **(U)** Pete Williams, Richard Esposito, Michael Isikoff, and Tracy Connor, "3 Pals of Boston Marathon Bombing Suspect Charged with Coverup," *NBC News*, May 1, 2013. (Available at: http://usnews.nbcnews.com/news/2013/05/01/18001437-3-pals-of-boston-marathon-bombing-suspect-charged-with-coverup?lite)

[84] **(U)** United States District Court, District of Massachusetts, "United States of America v. Dias Kadyrbayev (1) Azamat Tazhayakov (2), and Robel Kidane Phillipos (3), Defendants," Case 1:13-cr-10238-DPW

[85] **(U)** Scott Neuman, "Kazakh Students Indicted in Boston Bombing Probe," *National Public Radio*, August 8, 2013. (Available at: http://www.npr.org/blogs/thetwo-way/2013/08/08/210211834/kazakh-students-indicted-in-boston-bombing-probe)

[86] **(U)** Associated Press, "Boston Arrest Prompts Homeland Security to Verify All Student Visas," *the Guardian*, May 3, 2013. (Available at: http://www.theguardian.com/world/2013/may/03/boston-marathon-bombings-arrest-student-visa)

[87] **(U)** Ibid.

committed a triple homicide on September 11, 2011.[88] While being questioned, Ibragim Todashev was shot and killed when he reportedly attacked FBI investigators.

(U)The bodies of Brendan Mess, Erik Weissman, and Raphael Teken were discovered in three different rooms of Mess' apartment on the morning of September 12, 2011, with their throats slit, and covered in marijuana and cash.[89] The three were all involved in martial arts, and Tamerlan Tsarnaev once reportedly described Brendan Mess as his "best friend."[90] One local investigator later noted that the brutality of the murders was perhaps the worst he'd seen in his career, and "their throats were slashed right out of an al Qaeda training video."[91] The motives for the killings remain unclear, though the symbolism of the date and the religion of the victims, at least two of whom were Jewish, raised media speculation that the murder was ideologically driven.[92]

(U) Born in Grozny, the capital of Chechnya, Ibragim Todashev came to the United States in 2008.[93] He is reported to have been friends with Tamerlan Tsarnaev, and the two trained in martial arts together.[94] Uncertainty still surrounds public accounts of the 2011 murder, yet Ibragim Todashev reportedly acknowledged he and Tamerlan Tsarnaev were responsible shortly before his death.[95] Briefings provided to the Committee by Federal officials indicate that authorities do not suspect he was at all connected to the Boston Marathon bombing. The DOJ and the Office of the State Attorney for the Ninth Judicial Circuit Court of Florida are each conducting reviews of the May 22, 2013 shooting of Ibragim Todashev by an FBI agent. At the time this report was finalized, these reviews were ongoing.

---

[88] (U) Michael S. Schmitt, William Rashbaum, and Richard A. Oppel, Jr., "Deadly End to FBI Queries on Tsarnaev and a Triple Killing," *the New York Times*, May 22, 2013. (Available at: http://www.nytimes.com/2013/05/23/us/officer-involved-in-shooting-of-man-tied-to-tsarnaev.html?hp&_r=0)

[89] (U) Alana Samuels, "Dead Boston Bombing Suspect Tsarnaev Tied to Gruesome Triple Homicide," *Los Angeles Times*, October 23, 2013. (Available at: http://www.latimes.com/nation/nationnow/la-na-nn-boston-triple-homicide-20131023,0,3300971.story#axzz2jDV9WYb6)

[90] (U) Michael Rezendes and Bob Hohlder, "Link Sought Between Brother, 3 Waltham killings," *the Boston Globe*, April 22, 2013. (Available at: http://www.bostonglobe.com/metro/2013/04/22/police-probe-possible-link-between-marathon-bomber-and-unsolved-triple-homicide-waltham/R9yUVyK2tVXxcoPEj2yvAP/story.html)

[91] (U) Michele McPhewe, "Boston Bomb Suspect Eyed in Connection to 2011 Triple Murder," *ABC News*, April 22, 2013. (Available at: http://abcnews.go.com/Blotter/boston-bomb-suspect-eyed-connection-2011-triple-murder/story?id=19015628)

[92] (U) David Frum, "Did Tamerlan Tsarnaev Kill his Jewish Friends?" *the Daily Beast*, April 24, 2013. (Available at: http://www.thedailybeast.com/articles/2013/04/24/did-tamerlan-tsarnaev-kill-his-jewish-friends.html)

[93] (U) Mark Hosenball, Barbara Liston, Thomas Grove, "Father of Chechen shot by FBI says he thinks son was tortured," *Reuters*, May 23, 2013. (Available at: http://www.reuters.com/article/2013/05/23/us-usa-explosion-chechnya-idUSBRE94M11320130523)

[94] (U) Susan Zalkind, "New Details in the FBI Shooting Death of Tamerlan Tsarnaev Associate," *Boston Magazine*, September 20, 2013. (Available at: http://www.bostonmagazine.com/news/blog/2013/09/20/new-details-fbi-shooting-death-tamerlan-tsarnaev-associate/)

[95] (U) Michael S. Schmitt, William Rashbaum, and Richard A. Oppel, Jr., *supra* note 88.

V.

(U) OVERSIGHT

(U) On April 20, 2013, the Committee sent the first of several letters to the FBI, DHS, and the ODNI in response to the death of Tamerlan Tsarnaev and the public announcement that he and his brother were suspects in the Boston Marathon bombing investigation.[96] This letter requested "all information and records" relating to Tamerlan Tsarnaev held by the U.S. Government. Again, on April 27, 2013, the Committee sent the same three Federal agencies a detailed series of questions regarding Tamerlan Tsarnaev's history, based on what was appearing in public media reporting about his life and interactions with the Federal Government. In early May, the Committee received a response from the legislative affairs representatives from FBI, DHS, and DNI indicating those agencies would not provide answers to the Committee. Intent to move forward in this investigation, however, the Committee convened its first hearing on the Boston Marathon Bombings to hear from local law enforcement officials of Boston and the Commonwealth of Massachusetts, as well as other experts.

(U) The Executive Branch supplied initial briefings on the bombings to all Members of Congress, and another to select representatives from the staffs of various Congressional Committees. It was argued, after the fact, in a May 5, 2013 response to the Committee that these meetings, and some brief phone conversations between the Committee and senior FBI leadership, should be considered enough to satisfy the Committee's inquiry. However, there remained significant gaps in the information supplied, and notes of these meetings were never made available for review or verification. The Committee informed the FBI, DHS, and ODNI that this was insufficient via a letter on May 15, 2013. Representatives from FBI and DHS offered the Committee a classified briefing to discuss the Committee's questions. In mid-June 2013 DHS provided briefings at length to answer the Committee's questions. The FBI declined to participate, citing bureau policy that prohibits providing "sworn testimony" in reference to ongoing prosecutions. However, on May 16, 2013 and again on June 19, 2013, then-FBI Director Mueller discussed the Boston attack in public testimony before the Senate.

(U) On June 12, 2013, the Committee extended a formal invitation to the FBI, DHS, and the NCTC (as an agency within the ODNI) to provide official testimony in a classified portion of the Committee's second hearing on the bombings. NCTC Director Olsen and then-DHS Principal Deputy Coordinator for Counterterrorism Cohen appeared before the Committee.[97] The FBI again declined citing the ongoing prosecution of Dzhokhar Tsarnaev. On June 14, 2013, the Committee notified the FBI of the Chairman's decision to conduct a site visit to Boston and

---

[96] (U) This letter, along with subsequent correspondence between the Committee and the FBI, DHS, and the ODNI (specifically the NCTC) are provided as an appendix to this report.

[97] (U) Mr. Cohen is now the Department's Counterterrorism Coordinator.

requested a meeting with FBI representatives from the Boston JTTF. After some deliberation, the FBI made SAC DesLauriers available for a meeting with Members of the Committee and local law enforcement hosted by the BPD.

(U) On July 3, 2013, the FBI wrote the Committee to reiterate their refusal to satisfy the Committee's inquiry. Despite the letter's assertion that briefing the Committee on this issue could potentially damage the FBI's own investigation and prosecution of the bombing, the Committee's requests in this matter have all focused on documents and information relating to Tamerlan Tsarnaev, not his brother Dzhokhar Tsarnaev. As he died in the early hours of April 19, 2013, supplying the necessary records on Tamerlan Tsarnaev would not damage the integrity of any future prosecution. Further, this letter attempted to argue that the FBI's interpretation of congressional jurisdiction released them from their obligation to answer the Committee's questions, and referred to the Committee's investigation as "non-oversight" activities.

(U) However, in September and October 2013, during a series of meetings with the Committee, FBI officials indicated a willingness to "reset" relations and begin cooperating with the Committee's investigation. In November 2013, a bi-partisan delegation of Committee staff traveled to meet with U.S. officials stationed at the U.S. Embassies in Moscow and Tbilisi. This delegation spoke with officials from DHS, FBI, and other agencies to further the Committee's investigation (among other issues). Subsequently, on November 21, 2013, Committee staff visited the Boston JTTF to meet with FBI investigators. These conversations with officials in Boston and Moscow provided extremely useful information and valuable perspective to the Committee's review. The information received has been incorporated into this report and the Committee will continue to build on these positive developments.

(U) Rule X, Clause 3 g(1) of the adopted rules of the House of Representatives makes clear that the Committee "shall review and study on a continuing basis all Government activities relating to homeland security...." This provides the Committee the jurisdiction to carry out this investigation, and request documents and information regarding Tamerlan Tsarnaev, and does not give any Executive Branch agency license to ignore this oversight effort.

(U) Initial reluctance to assist the Committee in this investigation was unfortunate because it is another example of problems identified in the 9/11 Commission Report that have yet to be solved. The Commission urged a "unity of effort in the Congress," and specifically noted that "Congress should create a single, principal point of oversight and review for homeland security."[98] This call was answered in part when the Committee was established as a standing committee. Though there are additional oversight recommendations in the 9/11 Commission Report which remain unfulfilled, the Committee takes its jurisdiction in this area seriously, and will continue to provide this oversight. A rejection of this Committee's effort is a reversion to a pre-9/11 mindset, and demonstrates a concerning disinterest in aiding Congress in improving our homeland security.

---

[98] (U) "The Complete 9/11 Commission Report," *National Commission on Terrorist Attacks Upon the United States*, July 26, 2004. Page 421

VI.

(U) FINDINGS AND RECOMMENDATIONS

(U) *Cooperation with Local Law Enforcement*

(U) On May 9, 2013, BPD Commissioner Edward Davis testified before the Committee that neither he, nor the wider Boston Police Department, were alerted to the potential threat that Tamerlan Tsarnaev posed either before, during, or after the Boston JTTF's 2011 assessment of Tamerlan Tsarnaev:

> ***Chairman McCaul.*** *Before the bombing were you aware that based on this Russian intelligence, the FBI opened an investigation into Tamerlan?*
> ***Commissioner Davis.*** *We were not aware of that.*
> ***Chairman McCaul.*** *Would you have liked to have known that?*
> ***Commissioner Davis.*** *Yes*
> ***Chairman McCaul.*** *Before the bombing were you aware that Mr. Tamerlan travelled to the Chechen region?*
> ***Commissioner Davis.*** *No, we were not.*
> ***Chairman McCaul.*** *Again, would you have liked to have known that?*
> ***Commissioner Davis.*** *Yes.*[99]

(U) The BPD had officers assigned to the Boston JTTF. However, existing agreements between the FBI and partner agencies required FBI approval before Task Force Officers (TFOs) could be share information with their parent agencies. The Committee has found similar prohibitions on sharing information across the country. In fact, this requirement is a staple of the Memoranda of Understanding (MOUs) signed between the FBI and other Federal, State, and local entities that are assigning personnel to a JTTF.[100]

(U) Though Commissioner Davis raised these concerns, it should be noted that he also stated the BPD may not have done anything differently based on the reporting from the Russian government.[101, 102] This provides valuable perspective, but as the Committee has indicated

---

[99] **(U)** Commissioner Edward Davis, "House Homeland Security Committee Holds Hearing on the Boston Terrorist Bombings," *CQ Congressional Transcripts*, May 9, 2013. (Available at: http://www.cq.com/doc/congressionaltranscipts-4272296)

[100] **(U)** At the request of the FBI, the Committee notes that the overall structure of the JTTF model is not in question.

[101] **(U)** Commissioner Edward Davis, *supra* note 99.

[102] **(U)** Additionally, given that Tamerlan Tsarnaev resided in the Boston suburb of Cambridge, it should be noted that this falls outside BPD's official jurisdiction.

several times in this report and throughout this investigation, it is impossible to know how wider dissemination may have impacted events.

(U) Even more critical is the fact that while nothing may have been done differently in this case, this is only one example of the wider information sharing relationship. Ensuring this relationship operates effectively at all times is paramount.

(U) This restriction runs counter to the claims that JTTFs are "one-stop shopping for information regarding terrorist activities," or that they "enable a shared intelligence base across many agencies."[103] As investigative bodies, JTTFs bring the expertise of several agencies under one roof to combat terror threats, but in this case, and possibly in others, the information they possessed may have been valuable when shared with other agencies. As former Mayor of New York Rudy Giuliani explained in testimony before the Committee, sharing information outside of the JTTF with local law enforcement about terrorist threats can help investigators:

(U) *But there's a second reason why the Boston Police should have been notified. And it wasn't just to notify the Boston Police, it was to ask for help. If the FBI receives notification from the government of Russia that a man is a suspected terrorist, and the FBI doesn't know if the man is a suspected terrorist or not, but has to investigate this, where would you go immediately? Where should you go immediately to get information about that, but to the police department where this man lives? Not just to notify them, to to ask for their help. To ask them for all the information they have about him, to ask them to put him under surveillance, to ask them to watch them.*[104]

(U) Mayor Giuliani estimated that there are "only about 12,000 to 13,000 FBI agents for the entire world," and that the FBI faces a diverse threat with limited resources. However, with proper training, Mayor Giuliani notes that the roughly 800,000 police officers around the country can assist the FBI in protecting the United States against terrorist attacks.[105] There is every indication that the 2011 assessment done on Tamerlan Tsarnaev by the Boston JTTF was thorough, and exhausted all options available to investigators at that time. However, Mayor Giuliani raises important issues about the most effective relationship between Federal investigators and local law enforcement more broadly.

(U) *Recommendation 1 – Increase Information Sharing with Local Law Enforcement*

(U) In examining the Boston Marathon bombing, the Committee strongly recommends finding ways to increase and enhance the information sharing between Federal intelligence and

---

[103] (U) "Protecting America from Terrorist Attack: Our Joint Terrorism Task Forces," *the Federal Bureau of Investigation.* (Available at: http://www.fbi.gov/about-us/investigate/terrorism/terrorism_jttfs)

[104] (U) Hon. Rudy Giuliani, "House Homeland Security Committee Holds Hearing on Assessing Attacks on the U.S. from Fort Hood to Boston, Panel 1," *CQ Congressional Transcripts,* July 10, 2013. (Available at: http://www.cq.com/doc/congressionaltranscripts-4312003)

[105] (U) Ibid.

law enforcement agencies and State, local, and Tribal law enforcement agencies. Based on official testimony provided during open hearings by current and former government officials, briefings with State and local law enforcement personnel and even the recommendations of representatives from Federal agencies including the National Counterterrorism Center (NCTC), the Committee has determined there is extensive room for improvement to be made in both the perception of the FBI's information sharing expectations of its agents and TFOs, as well as the actual information sharing procedures in place. Moving forward, the Committee hopes that more information can be shared beyond JTTFs around the country with State and local police departments relating to such ongoing assessments.

(U) This includes expanding access to classified networks such as Guardian at the various State and local fusion centers. The Guardian system "serves as the primary database for setting leads to other Field Offices and JTTFs to open new terrorism related assessments or investigations,"[106] and a Guardian lead was initiated for Tamerlan Tsarnaev based on the liaison memorandum from the Russian government. In a briefing provided to Committee Staff, DHS Coordinator for Counterterrorism John Cohen noted that while fusion centers have access to eGuardian,[107] DHS is working with the FBI to explore increasing the number of persons on Fusion Centers with access to Guardian itself.[108] Concern regarding state and local access to classified material was echoed by several local law enforcement officials during the course of the Committee's investigation, who suggested that improvements could also be made to the timeliness of threat reporting made available to fusion centers and police departments. It has been argued that some fusion centers have access to Guardian by virtue of individuals who serve both as part of the center and the local JTTF. Yet, this is not enough to ensure the fusion center has true Guardian access.

(U) Additionally, expanding access to the Guardian system is not the only way to increase information sharing between Federal and State and local partners. Ensuring leaders of major city police departments across the country have the necessary clearances to receive threat information, and developing policies that provide these individuals with insight into ongoing or closed JTTF investigations and assessments may also be effective in preparing local law enforcement for emerging threats within their communities. Furthermore, testimony provided to the Committee by Richard Stanek, Sheriff of Hennepin County, Minnesota during a hearing examining the threat of Westerners travelling abroad for training with al Qaeda, identified areas

---

[106] **(U)** Hon. William H. Webster, Douglas E. Winter, Adrian L. Steel, Jr. William M. Baker, Russell J. Bruemmer, and Kenneth L. Wainstein, "Final Report of the William H. Webster Commission on the Federal Bureau of Investigation, Counterterrorism Intelligence, and the Events at Fort Hood, Texas, on November 5, 2009," *the William H. Webster Commission*, July 19, 2012. (Available at: http://www.fbi.gov/news/pressrel/press-releases/judge-webster-delivers-webster-commission-report-on-fort-hood)

[107] **(U)** eGuardian is an *unclassified* threat reporting system similar to but distinct from the classified Guardian network.

[108] **(U)** DHS Briefings to Committee Staff, March 4, 2014

where Federal and State and local law enforcement could work more closely together.[109] Sheriff Stanek noted that police departments that detailed officers to the FBI for placement on a JTTF "would also like to see the security clearances maintained of JTTF task force officers, even after they rotated back to their home agency." This is a common sense change, because it will ensure institutional knowledge is built up in local law enforcement and, as the Sheriff later noted, because clearances are a significant investment.

(U) *Recommendation 2 – Revise Agreements on TFOs*

(U//FOUO) Throughout our examination of this attack, the Committee repeatedly learned of problems associated with the MOUs signed between partnering agencies and the FBI when assigning non-FBI personnel to Joint Terrorism Task Forces around the country. The Committee understands that as these problems have gained more attention, the FBI convened a working-group to revisit the MOUs and other information sharing issues associated with the JTTFs.[110] In a July 22, 2013 email provided to the Committee by the FBI, Deputy Director Sean Joyce acknowledged that "some TFOs have been led to believe that the provision of their JTTF MOU that requires supervisory (SSA) approval before FBI information is disseminated to their home agency is essentially a prohibition on information sharing."[111] Deputy Director Joyce goes on to clarify in a November 26, 2013 letter to the Major Cities Chiefs Association (MCCA) that, while a requirement for SSA approval on such sharing will remain a part of the MOUs "we have revised the language… to indicate that this requirement is not intended to dissuade the sharing of information."[112]

(U) It is the Committee's recommendation that these agreements foster a more open and collaborative relationship, where more TFOs can share information with their parent agency and local fusion centers, and the Committee views these changes as a step toward that end. Representatives from both local and Federal law enforcement have noted that there is risk in providing too much information to too many people. Potential leaks could damage the integrity of investigations, and possibly affect sources and methods of gathering threat information. Of course, limiting the flow of critical information also risks lives.

(U//FOUO) Similarly, as part of their response to this attack, the FBI has issued guidance to all members of JTTFs across the country that encourages them to collaborate and communicate

---

[109] (U) Richard Stanek, Tesimony before the U.S. House of Representatives Committee on Homeland Security, 113th Congress, First Session, October 9, 2013, "From al-Shabaab to al-Nusra: How Westerners Joining Terror Groups Overseas Affect the Homeland," Statement for the Record, Page 3.

[110] (U//FOUO) According to FBI officials in Boston, this group consisted of local law enforcement and FBI officials from across the United States.

[111] (U//FOUO) Deputy Director of the FBI Sean Joyce correspondence with Las Vegas Metropolitan Police Department Sheriff Douglas Gillespie, November 26, 2013 (provided to the Committee on December 16, 2013).

[112] (U//FOUO) Deputy Director of the FBI Sean Joyce correspondence with Las Vegas Metropolitan Police Department Sheriff Douglas Gillespie, November 26, 2013 (provided to the Committee on December 16, 2013).

between one another. This reminder seems to be targeted at ensuring that there is greater visibility within each task force of which assessments and investigations are ongoing. As Deputy Director Joyce notes in his correspondence with the MCCA, "state and local chiefs should encourage their TFOs to leverage their position on the JTTF to stay abreast of any threat or investigation...even if they are not directly assigned to the particular investigation in question."[113] The Committee feels this is a positive change, and recommends that this effort be reinforced with additional, permanent policy changes.

(U) *TECS Lookouts and Response*

(U) On November 6, 2011, Tamerlan Tsarnaev purchased a ticket to fly to Moscow from John F. Kennedy Airport in New York.[114] According to DHS, on January 18, 2012 – three days before his flight – the TECS system notified a CBP officer assigned to the Boston JTTF of the scheduled trip. This was the same CBP officer who had initially placed this alert on Tamerlan Tsarnaev during the 2011 assessment by the JTTF. Records demonstrate that this CBP officer did receive and view the alert, but official FBI and DHS accounts cannot officially verify whether the TECS alert was shared with the FBI case agent who led the 2011 assessment.[115] As a matter of policy, the FBI considers all individuals formally assigned to the JTTF as part of the FBI and acknowledges, therefore, that the JTTF was officially aware of Tamerlan Tsarnaev's plans to travel.[116]

(U//FOUO//LES) According to DHS, Tamerlan Tsarnaev's ticket was a one-way reservation scheduled for January 22, 2012.[117] The first TECS alert on Tamerlan Tsarnaev was placed on March 22, 2011.[118] His planned travel out of the country fell within a year of the date this alert was placed. ███ ██ As a result, in this case the CBP office at John F. Kennedy International Airport also received a list of passengers of concern for the date that Tamerlan Tsarnaev was travelling, which included his name.[119]

(U//FOUO//LES) ██ █████████████ On the date of Tamerlan Tsarnaev's travel, there were 22 CBP officers assigned

---

[113] (U//FOUO) Deputy Director of the FBI Sean Joyce correspondence with Las Vegas Metropolitan Police Department Sheriff Douglas Gillespie. November 26, 2013 (provided to the Committee on December 16, 2013).

[114] (U) DHS Briefings to Committee Staff, March 4, 2014

[115] (U) DHS Briefings to Committee Staff, March 4, 2014

[116] (U) DHS Briefings to Committee Staff, March 4, 2014

[117] (U) DHS Briefings to Committee Staff, June 2013.

[118] (U) DHS Briefings to Committee Staff, March 4, 2014

[119] (U) CBP Briefing to Committee Staff, December 11, 2013.

[120] (U) CBP Briefing to Committee Staff, December 11, 2013.

to conduct outbound targeting and examinations for the five international terminals at John F. Kennedy International Airport. Further details are needed to conclude whether these resources were sufficient to review all individuals of interest travelling out of JFK that day. However, at this point, it appears that guidance issued to CBP officials to prioritize these reviews was a key factor in the decision not to review the records of all names ████████████ The Committee has requested that the Government Accountability Office (GAO) conduct a review of this process to fully evaluate these issues.

(U) There is no indication that CBP officials at the John F. Kennedy International Airport reviewed the record related to Tamerlan Tsarnaev. CBP Officials indicated in a briefing with Committee staff that this was likely because of how Tamerlan Tsarnaev's alert was coded (he was not placed on the No Fly list) and particularly that, without comment from the JTTF (which the CBP officials at the point of exit did not receive), they would not normally conduct such an examination.[121] Given the volume of passengers travelling into and out of the United States on any given day, ensuring all individuals of concern are examined is, and always will be, a challenge. Adequate resources for CBP to carry out this mission are vital, and CBP officials indicated that outbound examinations are prioritized to those passengers who pose the most risk. As there was no communication from the Boston JTTF to CBP officials at the point of departure to conduct additional screening, CBP did not feel Tamerlan Tsarnaev warranted this additional scrutiny.

(U//FOUO//LES) However, the TECS record entered on March 22, 2011 is unequivocal in its request for Tamerlan Tsarnaev to receive secondary screening – and this did not factor into the CBP's prioritization. CBP officials reported to the Committee that there is no record that the CBP officials ████████████████ examined Tamerlan Tsarnaev's TECS record and therefore did not see that request.

(U//FOUO//LES) Upon his return from Russia six months later, Tamerlan Tsarnaev's TECS alert once again notified the record-holder of his intended travel.[122] Tamerlan's return was booked on June 22, 2012 and he departed on July 17, 2012.[123] Once again, neither DHS nor FBI can verify from written or electronic records if this information was passed on from the CBP officer on the Boston JTTF to his colleagues, and in particular the Case Agent. Also, ████████ ███ the record did not alert CBP officers at the John F. Kennedy International Airport of Tamerlan's return and he was not given secondary screening when his flight landed.[124] These TECS alerts presented multiple potential opportunities to advance the FBI's understanding of Tamerlan Tsarnaev and the threat he posed.

---

[121] (U) DHS Briefings to Committee Staff, June 2013.

[122] (U) DHS Briefings to Committee Staff, March 4, 2014.

[123] (U) DHS Briefings to Committee Staff, June 2013.

[124] (U) The Committee will elaborate on the value of secondary screening and the additional opportunities for Tamerlan Tsarnaev to be screened upon his return below.

(U) A copy of the letter sent by the Russian government to the FBI regarding Tamerlan Tsarnaev specifically requested that the FBI notify Russia if Tamerlan decided to travel.[125] The agents and TFOs on the Boston JTTF assigned to carry out an assessment of Tamerlan in 2011 should have been familiar with this request. Though the Committee understands that the TECS alert was not placed in response to this request, the fact that Tamerlan Tsarnaev did fulfill this warning ought to have warranted greater examination by the FBI when he returned. However, FBI Officials have stressed that knowledge of Tamerlan Tsarnaev's travel, by itself, would not be sufficient predicate to reopen the 2011 assessment or expand it to a preliminary investigation. In this context, opportunities to collect additional information are all the more important.

(U) The FBI's 2011 assessment concluded Tamerlan Tsarnaev did not have links to terrorism. 14 months later, after his return from Russia he began to post extremist-themed videos, and later disrupted services at his mosque. A second assessment or even the decision to expand into a preliminary investigation after Tamerlan Tsarnaev's return could potentially have yielded evidence to suggest that he had been radicalized. While it is impossible to say with certainty that such a second look would have prevented the bombings, it is equally impossible to say with certainty it could not have.

(U) *Recommendation 3 – Secondary Examinations*

(U//FOUO//LES) As noted above, CBP prioritizes the review of records for outgoing international travelers before they depart the United States if a TECS alert is triggered. In this case, because Tamerlan Tsarnaev's name was associated with an active TECS alert at the time he left John F. Kennedy International Airport for Moscow, he was initially placed on a list of travelers of interest departing the United States that day. It is disconcerting that a decision was made not to review the TECS files for all of those individuals ▮▮▮▮▮▮▮ – especially in the absence of additional communication from the JTTF. The Committee was pleased to learn that in the aftermath of the bombing, CBP issued guidance to the field mandating the review of all possible matches. CBP reports they also subsequently enhanced system functionality to facilitate the review requirements. Ports of entry remain responsible for prioritizing their identification of subjects that pose the highest level of potential threat (while taking into account the scheduled departure time). This is a positive step, but additional concerns remain.

(U//FOUO//LES) The Committee strongly recommends increasing the examination of international travelers with such alerts on their name as they depart the country. Furthermore, the Committee recommends finding ways to allow for the examination of all individuals whose status causes them to be selected ▮▮▮▮▮▮ This will pose a challenge given the current fiscal environment and tightening budgets across Federal agencies, but is another avenue to strengthen the security of the United States. In working to address this and other challenges faced by CBP, the Committee is gravely concerned by continued leadership vacancies in that agency

---

[125] **(U)** This copy was made available for the Committee to review, but not retain, by the House of Representatives' Committee on the Judiciary.

and across DHS, which will slow or prohibit the Department's continued evolution into a more effective entity.

(U) *Recommendation 4 – Improving TECS Alert Notifications and Records*

(U) Since former Secretary of Homeland Security Janet Napolitano's report that the system "pinged" when Tamerlan Tsarnaev left the United States for Russia, attention has turned to the TECS alert placed on his name as part of the 2011 assessment carried out by the Boston JTTF.[126] Yet beyond a record of the TECS alert notifying the CBP Officer who initially placed this alert that Tamerlan Tsarnaev was leaving, it is not clear that this information was shared with others on the Boston JTTF. The Committee recommends ensuring that the FBI Case Agents on each assessment where a TECS alert is placed on an individual also receives these notifications, and that each time a TECS alert is shared there is a written record to detail when, how, and with whom this alert is communicated. The Committee understands it is possible (and even likely) that this alert, and the alert that was sent upon Tamerlan Tsarnaev's return were shared verbally with others on the Boston JTTF, yet the absence of a reliable record that demonstrates this makes it difficult to know with certainty who was aware that Tamerlan was travelling.

(U) CBP has informed the Committee that they have worked to address this recommendation. On May 2013, guidance was issued to the field that all CBP officers assigned to JTTFs notify the FBI Case Agent upon identification of any international travel for subjects of interest not listed in the TSDB, via government email systems. In addition to other forms of communication, the email correspondence will provide a record of these notifications for future reference. The Committee also recommends finding ways to automate this process and reduce the possibility for human error in ensuring these records are shared.

(U) *Nomination for TIDE/TSDB and the Second TECS Alert*

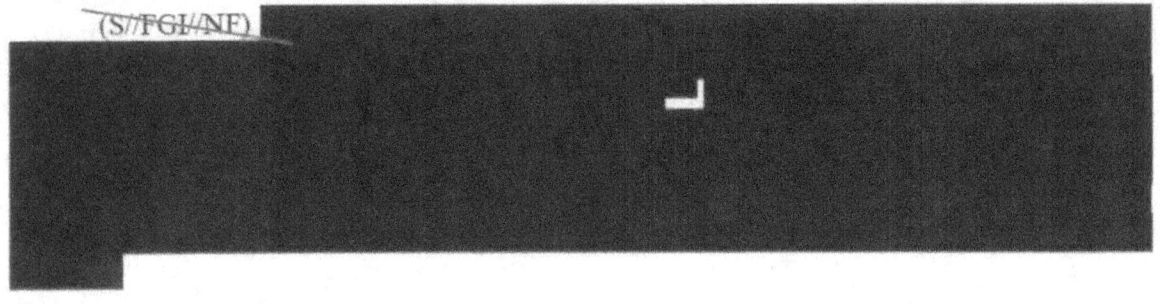

(S//FGI//NF)

---

[126] **(U)** "'System Pinged" When Boston Bombing Suspect Went to Russia, Napolitano Says," *CNS News*, April 23, 2013. (Available at: http://www.cbsnews.com/video/watch/?id=50145465n)

[127] (S//FGI//NF

However, these alerts were not identical, and remained distinct from one another. Specifically, Tamerlan Tsarnaev's name spelling and date of birth were inaccurate, and as a result there was no match through TIDE [Terrorist Identities Datamart Environment]..[130] In TECS records provided to the Committee, an alert entered on October 20, 2011 spells Tamerlan Tsarnaev's surname as "Tsarnayev," and lists his birthday in 1987 instead of 1986. Just as the FBI's TECS alert was unambiguous in its requests, this second TECS alert specifically requested that officials encountering Tamerlan Tsarnaev "Escort [him] to CBP secondary and detain is mandatory whether or not the officer believes there is an exact match." It is disturbing that such a detailed lookout could be missed, either because the TECS system did not connect the erroneous TECS alert with the real Tamerlan Tsarnaev,

The FBI was unable to nominate Tamerlan Tsarnaev for TIDE or TSDB because to do so would have required expanding the 2011 assessment into a preliminary investigation, which investigators concluded they did not have sufficient evidence to do.[133]

(U) Maintained by the NCTC, TIDE consists of, "all information the USG [United States Government] possesses related to the identities of individuals known or appropriately suspected to be or to have been involved in activities constituting, in preparation for, in aid of, or related to terrorism (with the exception of purely domestic terrorism information)."[134] Agencies nominate individuals for TIDE through the NCTC, and in turn these records can be added to additional Federal terrorist "watchlists," if they meet the necessary threshold. The NCTC can then provide an unclassified version of these records to the Terrorist Screening Center (TSC), which maintains the TSDB.[135]

---

[128] (U) The TECS alert placed by the CIA was established on October 20, 2011.

[129] (U) DHS Briefings to Committee Staff, March 4, 2014.

[130] (U) DHS Briefings to Committee Staff, March 4, 2014.

[131] (U) In regard to the failure of automated systems to identify these records as referring to the same person, CBP reports that on May 9, 2013, they "fully deployed Russian-IBM regularization in its Global Name Recognition (GNR) application."

[132] (U) DHS Briefings to Committee Staff, March 4, 2014.

[133] (U) FBI briefing for Committee Staff, February 3, 2014.

[134] (U) "Terrorist Identities Datamart Environment (TIDE)" *the National Counterterrorism Center*. (Available at: http://nctc.gov/docs/Tide_Fact_Sheet.pdf)

[135] (U) "Terrorist Screening Center: Frequently Asked Questions," *the Federal Bureau of Investigation*.

[REDACTED]¹³⁶ As noted, Tamerlan Tsarnaev's name and birth date were inaccurate, as well. At this time, the NCTC informed the FBI that Tamerlan Tsarnaev had been nominated for TIDE via the FBI's Foreign Terrorism Tracking Force. However, they did not ask the FBI, nor did the FBI volunteer, to add all of the information in their records on Tamerlan to the TIDE/TSDB record on Tamerlan Tsarnaev, or to correct the spelling of his name or his date of birth.

(U//FOUO//LES) Because the two TECS alerts on his name were not identical, and because the TSDB record for him was incomplete and inaccurate, Tamerlan Tsarnaev did not receive a secondary examination as he returned to the United States from Russia.[137] [REDACTED]

[REDACTED] Given his interest in jihadist materials, it is possible CBP officials might have found something in his possession that would have revealed the threat he posed. This lack of communication represents a failure to proactively share information that could potentially save lives. Indeed, any further scrutiny upon Tamerlan Tsarnaev's return from Russia might have prevented the bombing if it revealed evidence of his radicalization or of ties to terrorism.

(U) *Recommendation 5 – Reviewing TSDB Nominations*

(U) A more accurate and complete TSDB record for Tamerlan Tsarnaev might have subjected him to greater scrutiny upon his return to the United States. The Committee recommends that all relevant agencies comply with NCTC's requirements that sponsoring agencies include all identifying information in their nominations.

(U//FOUO//LES) Similarly, the Committee recommends changes to the TSDB nomination process that would require a third-party agency with information on an individual being nominated to proactively share corrections or additional information. In this case, the FBI was made aware of Tamerlan Tsarnaev's TIDE record, and had more accurate information (a correct name and date of birth) they did not share with the NCTC. Additionally, on August 6, 2013, both the NCTC and CBP signed a Letter of Intent to improve data sharing and record enhancement related to the watchlist. Particularly, according to CBP officials [REDACTED] [REDACTED], CBP, TSC, and NCTC are now able to automatically transmit data to quickly enhance TIDE/TSDB records."[138]

(U) *Addressing Long-Term Challenges*

---

[136] **(U)** DHS Briefings to Committee Staff, March 4, 2014

[137] (U) It should be noted that Tamerlan Tsarnaev's record was inaccurate in that the initial information was inaccurate, not because NCTC entered an incomplete or false record.

[138] **(U)** DHS, NCTC, and FBI Briefing to Committee Staff, December 16, 2013.

(U) The Boston Marathon bombing took place on Monday April 15, 2013. Sometime around or just shortly after midnight on Friday, April 19, 2013, investigators began to suspect that two individuals involved in a Cambridge, Massachusetts carjacking might be responsible for the bombing that took place some 82 hours prior. The victim, whom the Tsarnaev brothers had held hostage for a period of time, allegedly reported to police upon his escape that Tamerlan and Dzhokhar claimed responsibility for the bombings.[139] Still, the account of Watertown Police Officers who first encountered Tamerlan and Dzhokhar Tsarnaev makes clear they did not suspect the two brothers had committed the attack until the Tsarnaevs exchanged gunfire with law enforcement and detonated improvised explosives on the street.[140]

(U) Nonetheless, it was not until Tamerlan Tsarnaev's fingerprints were scanned that the identity of the attackers became known to authorities. It had been roughly three and a half days from the blasts near the finish line of the Boston Marathon, and almost nine hours since pictures of the suspects were made public by FBI SAC Deslauriers. In that time, not one associate of Tamerlan or Dzhokhar Tsarnaev identified them to the authorities. Members of Tamerlan's mosque, the ISB, did not identify him as the man they had thrown out months before for arguing with a preacher. Classmates and friends of Dzhokhar did not alert police that they recognized his face on TV. These inactions may have cost MIT Campus Police Officer Sean Collier his life.

(U) It is difficult to know exactly how many closed assessments or investigations from recent years the Boston JTTF had on April 15, 2013. Whatever the figure, it is difficult to credibly speculate that, in the wake of the bombing, each of these files could have been reexamined to look for potential new leads. Personnel from multiple agencies were pulled in several directions; whether it was exploiting evidence from the scene, reviewing witness accounts, or combing through the thousands of images and hours of video from the Boston Marathon to identify suspects.

(U) The Committee believes this massive effort is a testament to unequivocal need for a positive, effective relationship between Federal agencies and between Federal, State, and local authorities working to investigate and mitigate terrorist threats. Some of the areas which are most necessary in working toward that goal are the perceptions or attitudes among officials and investigators. In some ways, this is tied to the top-down guidance provided to individuals from each agency involved in a JTTF. In the Committee's investigation, much discussion has focused around existing perceptions of policy or roles and responsibilities. It is absolutely necessary for the leaders of our nation's counterterrorism efforts not to allow *mis*perceptions to limit their agencies' effectiveness – and working to communicate guidance to their personnel is paramount. The post-bombing guidance issued by FBI officials intended to clarify JTTF MOUs and other roles and responsibilities is an example of the type of instruction and management that must be continually evaluated, improved, and communicated to all counterterrorism partners.

---

[139] (U) Katharine Q. Seelya, William K. Rashbaum, and Michael Cooper, "2nd Bombing Suspect Caught After Frenzied Hunt Paralyzes Boston," *the New York Times*, April 20, 2013. (Available at: http://www.nytimes.com/2013/04/20/us/boston-marathon-bombings.html?pagewanted=1&_r=1&hp&)

[140] (U) Vincent DeWitt, *supra* note 69.

(U) *Recommendation 6 – Encouraging Cooperation and Assistance from the Community*

(U) When investigators were unable to locate the identities of the suspects that video evidence suggested had carried out the Boston Marathon bombing, they turned to the public for help. This public appeal for information regarding the suspects, who would later turn out to be Tamerlan and Dzhokhar Tsarnaev, was not without risk, yet presented the hope that someone who recognized the individuals in the photos would alert the authorities. Unfortunately, no one stepped forward. This failure to take responsibility ultimately cost lives, and the Committee recommends efforts to strengthen and expand DHS' "If You See Something, Say Something," program. Shortly before the attack in Boston, the DHS Center of Excellence at the University of Maryland (known as the National Consortium for the Study of Terrorism and Responses to Terrorism or START), released a report that demonstrated that 56% of the country had never heard of the "If you See Something, Say Something" campaign. Ensuring that Americans are alerting their local police or Federal authorities to suspicious behavior or other potential indicators is an important step in preventing terrorist attacks. Certainly, such public education programs will require continued evaluation to ensure they are effective. However, members of a local community are the individuals best placed to identify potential terrorist threats. Toward that end, nationwide efforts to combat radicalization, such as DHS' Countering Violent Extremism (CVE) strategy, should receive similarly increased scrutiny to evaluate efficacy.

(U) *Recommendation 7 – Ending the "Case Closed" Mentality*

(U) In testimony before Congress, then-FBI Director Robert Mueller noted that though there were problems with communications breakdowns between Federal investigators, he felt that, "even if [procedures] had been fixed prior to the Boston bombing, I do not think it would have stopped it."[141] Other unnamed FBI officials were more direct in noting that even if the FBI had known about Tamerlan Tsarnaev's travel, it would not have changed the outcome. One official is quoted as noting, "the FBI investigation into the individual in question had been closed six months prior to his departure... since there was no derogatory information, there was no reason to suggest that additional action was warranted."[142] In early August 2013, it was reported that the FBI had concluded an internal investigation into the incident and determined they could not have prevented the attack.[143] The Committee has been informed that while the FBI and other

---

[141] **(U)** Noah Bierman, "FBI Director Admits to Lapse Before Marathon Bombing," *The Boston Globe*, June 14, 2013. (Available at: http://www.bostonglobe.com/news/nation/2013/06/13/mueller-communication-flaw-preceded-marathon-bombing/KibendVxgl8xDkUiKEGp6l/story.html)

[142] **(U)** Greg Miller, "Anti-Terror Task Force Was Warned of Tamerlan Tsarnaev's Long Trip to Russia," The Washington Post, April 25, 2013. (Available at: http://www.washingtonpost.com/world/national-security/anti-terror-task-force-was-warned-of-tamerlan-tsarnaevs-long-trip-russia/2013/04/05/0ed426de-addb-11e2-8bf6-e70cb6ae066e_story.html)

[143] **(U)** Michael Schmitt, "FBI Said to Find It Could Not Have Averted Boston Attack," *The New York Times*, August 1, 2013. (Available at: http://www.nytimes.com/2013/08/02/us/fbi-said-to-conclude-it-could-not-have-averted-boston-attack.html?_r=0)

agencies have conducted multiple reviews related to this case, none has resulted in a formal report memorializing the relevant findings. Though a joint effort by the Inspectors General (IGs) of the Intelligence Community, Department of Justice, Department of Homeland Security, and the Central Intelligence Agency to look into this matter was announced on April 30, 2013, this effort is ongoing.

(U) The Committee is therefore concerned that officials are asserting that this attack could not have been prevented, without compelling evidence to confirm that is the case. This is perhaps the most difficult problem to address, but is extremely important and addressing it requires a delicate balance. Ensuring that our investigators and counterterrorism professionals are confident, yet appropriately critical, once again returns to themes identified in previous works, and in particular the 9/11 Commission Report. Again, the Committee repeats the warnings of the Commission and urges the men and women of our intelligence and law enforcement communities and their leadership to approach potential gaps with a critical eye and to be forthright with ways to address the challenges they face.